What is it?

Joan Loss

What is it?

A BOOK OF PHOTOGRAPHIC PUZZLERS

Doubleday & Company, Inc.   Garden City, New York

A note for photographers: A 35mm single-lens reflex camera was used with the close-ups taken through a standard 55mm lens mounted on a bellows attachment.

Library of Congress Cataloging in Publication Data

Loss, Joan.
  What is it?

  Summary: The reader is challenged to identify
close-up photographs of familiar objects found in
most homes shown here from ten to thirty times larger
than their real size.
  1. Macrophotography—Juvenile literature.
[1. Macrophotography] I. Title.
TR684.L67   778.3′1
ISBN 0-385-00396-X
     0-385-06703-8 (lib. bdg.)
Library of Congress Catalog Card Number 73-9038

To everyone who had a hand in this book

Can you guess what each object is in the following "close-up" photographs? All are things that can be found in most homes. They may be hard to recognize, though, because they are shown here from ten to thirty times larger than their real size.

To find out what each "close-up" is, turn the page and see if you have guessed correctly.

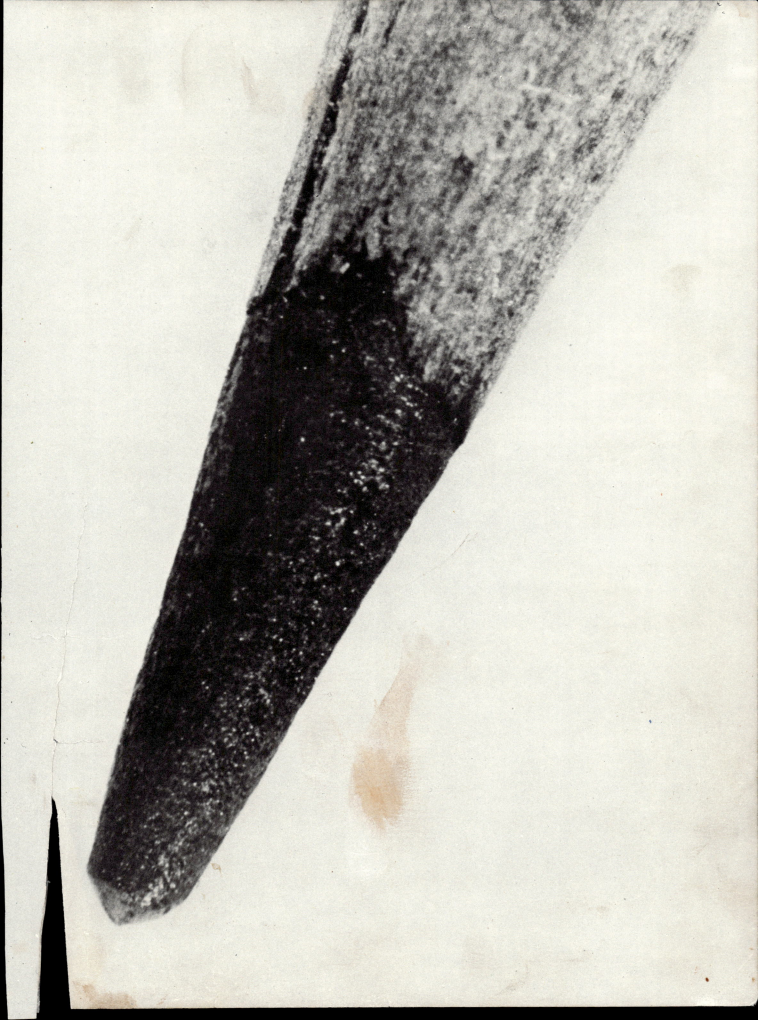

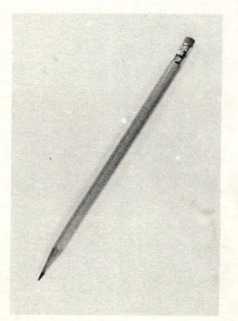

Pencil

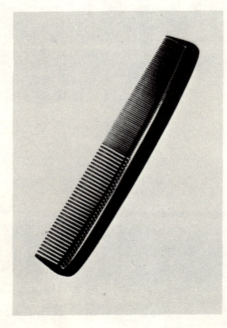

Comb

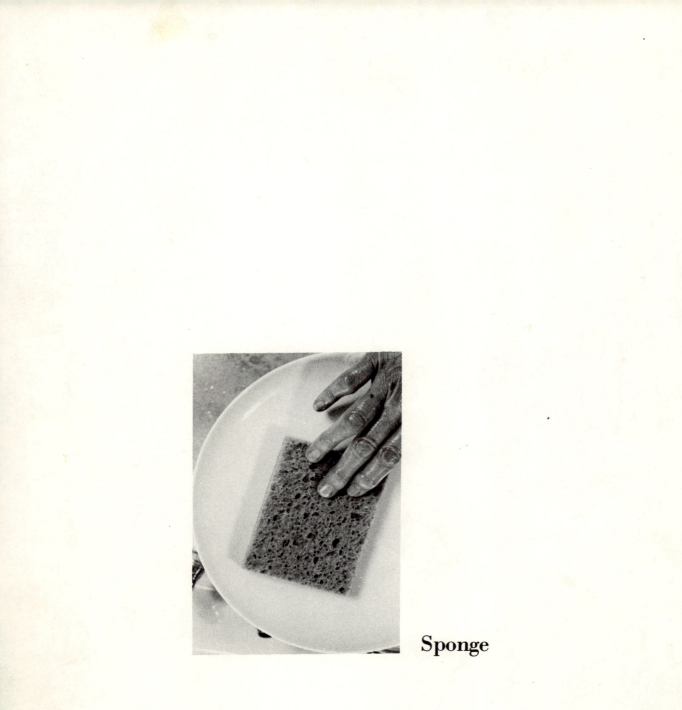

Sponge

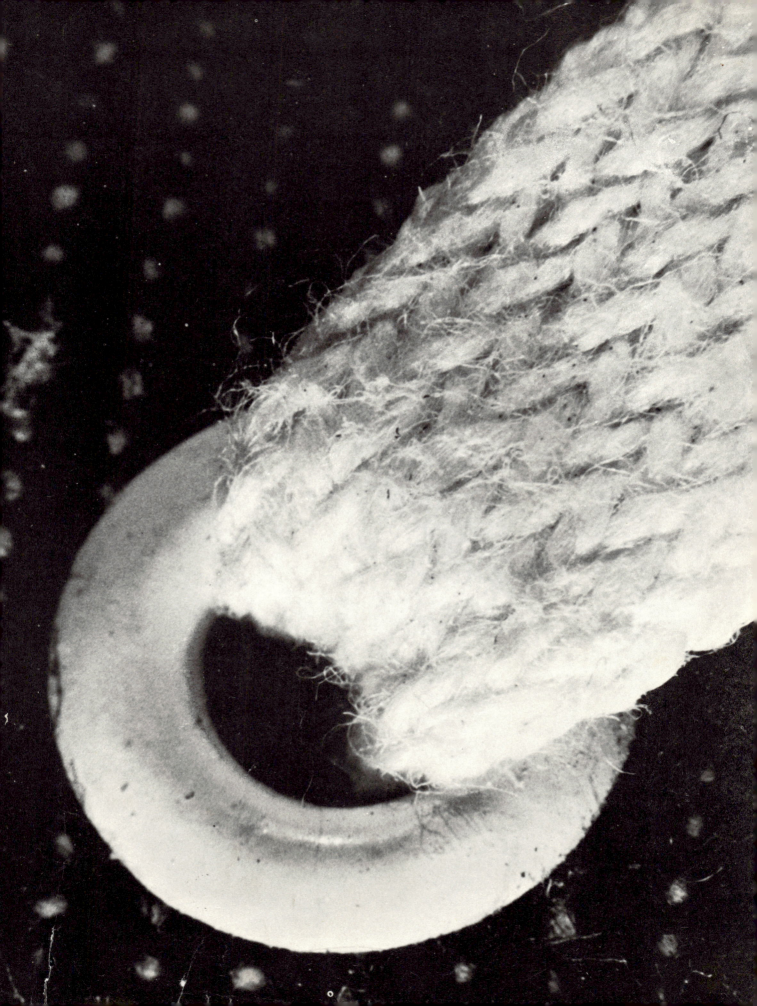

Sneaker shoelace

Zipper

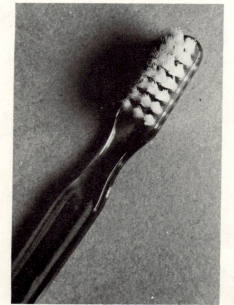

Toothbrush bristles

Toothpicks

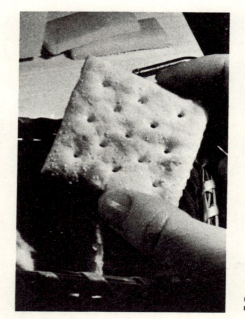

Saltine cracker

Terry cloth bath towel

24

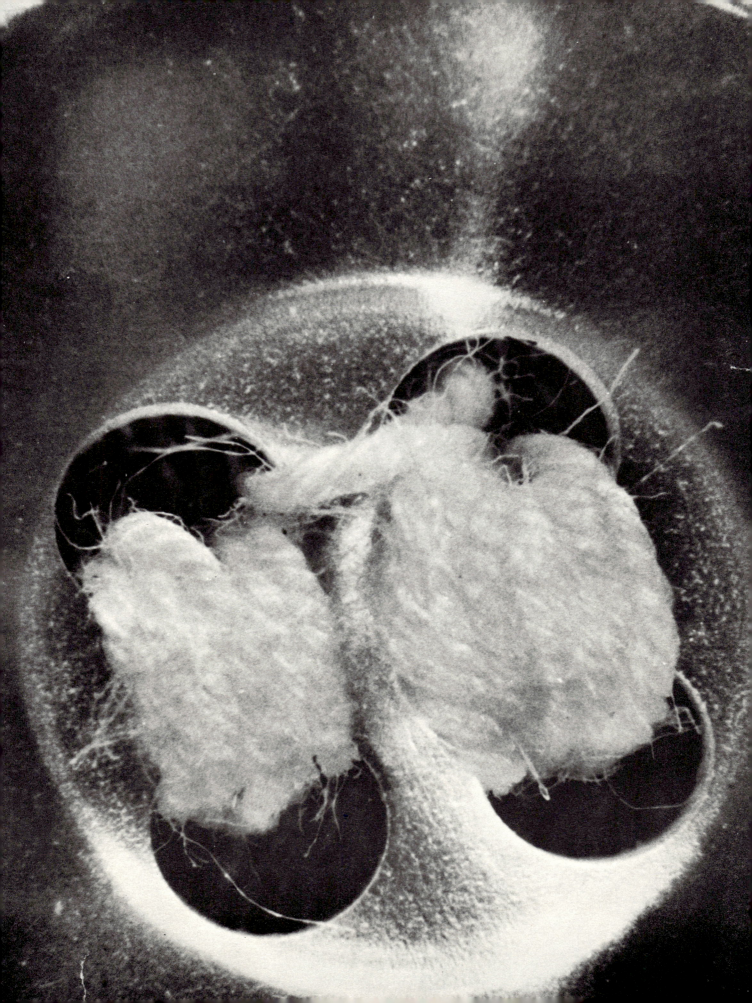

Button

Thumbtacks

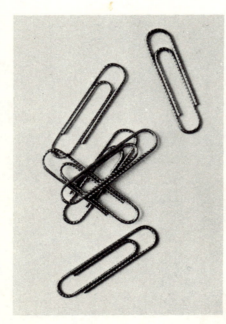

Paper clips

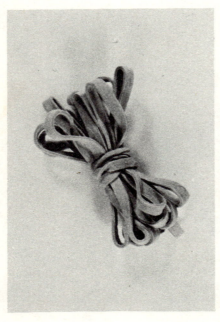

Rubber bands

Salt

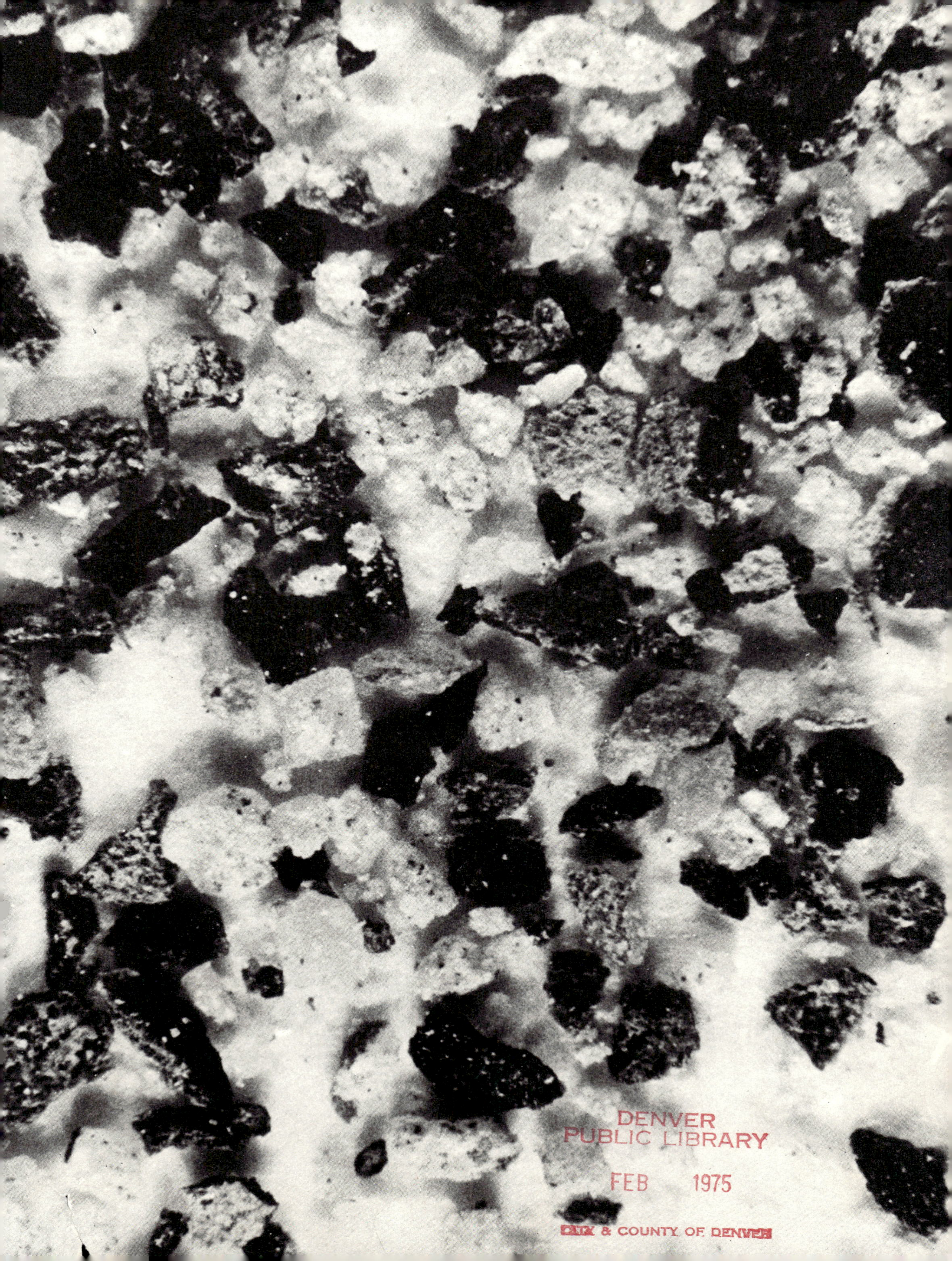

Pepper

Sugar

Book pages

Waffle

Harford Starts Dusting Off Summer Recreation Spots

Newspaper picture

From the *Evening Sun* (Baltimore, Maryland), 6/19/72, 5-star edition, page C4.

44

Scouring pad

46

About the Author

Joan Loss was born and grew up in the Baltimore, Maryland, area, where she still lives and works. She has been an elementary school teacher in the Baltimore County Board of Education and later became a librarian/audio-visual coordinator, a job in which her special interest in photography is most useful. Ms. Loss studied photography at the College of Art, Maryland Institute, where she learned how to develop and print her black-and-white pictures; her techniques and her eye for a fascinating shot are all self-taught.